Intro

This book is only a method on how to play guitar chords. My method is based on the success of my students that I have taught for twenty years at the Fine Arts association. Some methods may seem more sophisticated or complicated or overwhelming, but my method reduces the guitar playing to the simplest level

Even though you will not be playing the notes in this course the notes are very valuable if you want to play other music beside, folk, rock, pop or blues. So I suggest acquiring a book to learn the notes. For younger students I suggest Guitar for the small fry and for older students I like Belwins 21st Century guitar method.

Try not to get too tense and try too hard. Guitar playing is not helped by extra tension. Music is a serious art form but anxiety does not help your manual skills of playing. You have enough problems without adding the guitar to your list of worrries. Just put your fingers on the dots as the charts and DVD shows and have some fun.

When I first started taking lessons here is how guitar lessons were taught. You would be given a book with songs and sheet music and notes in it. You would look at the musical staff

and How Long the Note was held would be shown by what type of note it was Whole-4 beats   Half–2 beats   Quarter1 beat Eighth-Half Beat Where The Note was placed on the staff would determine what note to play Each individual note would be introduced. Then you would play songs like home on the range and twinkle little star.

Below are standard guitar chord charts. The lines down represent the guitar strings. The string on the right is your thinnest string and the string on the left is you're thickest. The dot is where you put your finger while the number is what finger to use. The piano fingering is 12345 while the guitar is thumb 1234. The x means do not hit the string.

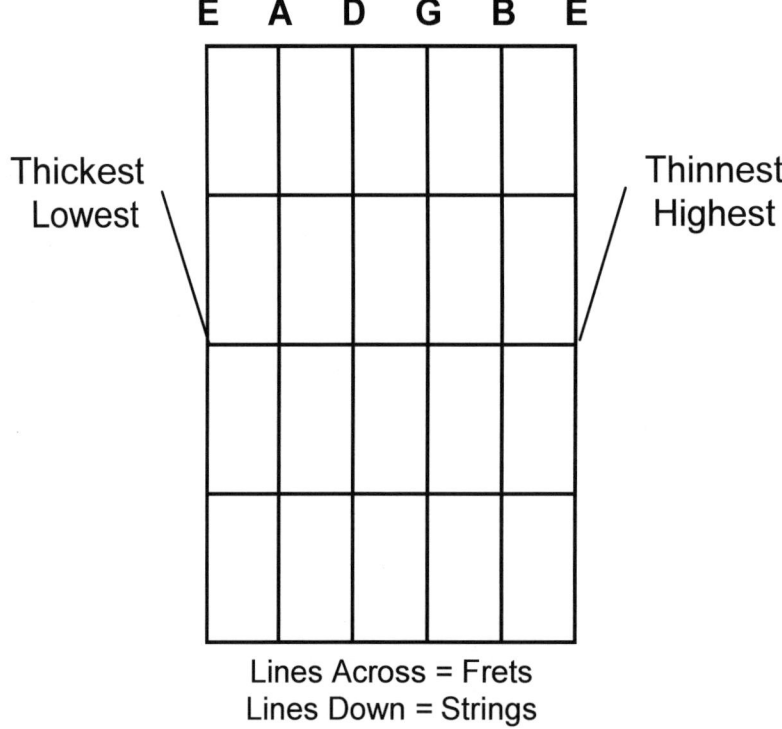

Now let's start strumming.

Lesson 2 C G

TRY THESE CHORDS STRUM STRAIGHT DOWN

SMALL C AND G

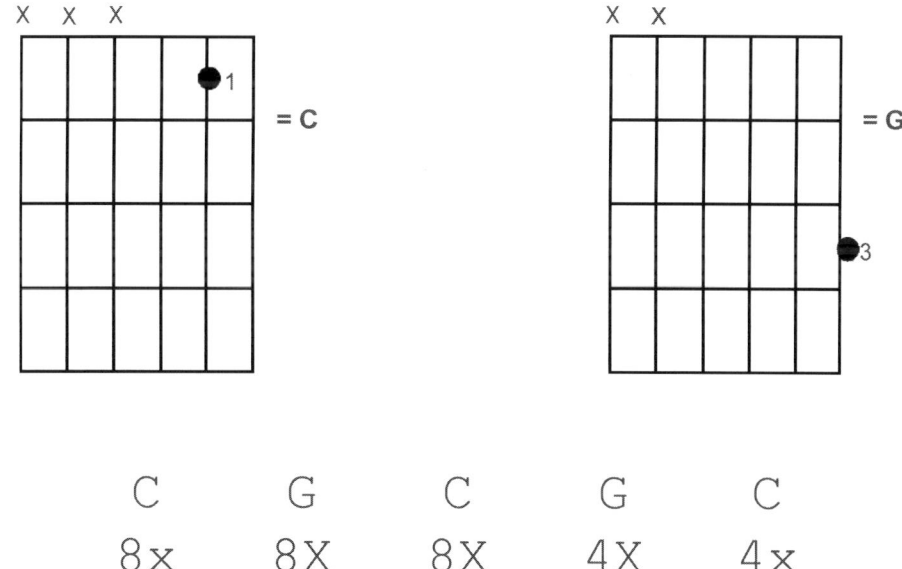

C	G	C	G	C
8x	8X	8X	4X	4x

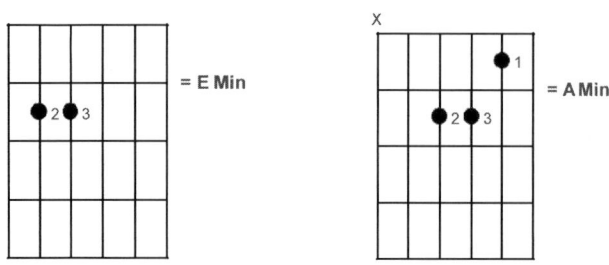

Lesson 3   Em Am

BE SURE AND DO THE CORRECT FINGERING ON THE EM ANDAM. See how easily with the correct fingering You Can learn these chords. Form theeminor then to make the amin move thesame chord form to the d and g strings andand then add the little C. Magic nowwe have 4 chords.

```
       Emin     Amin     emin
       4x       4x       4x
```

Lesson 4 Note Values

How Long the Note was held would be shown by what type of note it was

Whole-4 beats　　　　Half-2 beats

Quarter-1 beat　　　　Eighth-Half beat

Lesson 5

Let's try a strum with root note Arrow up means strum up. Arrow down means strum down

The six lines below represent your guitar strings. O means to hit the low E string open.

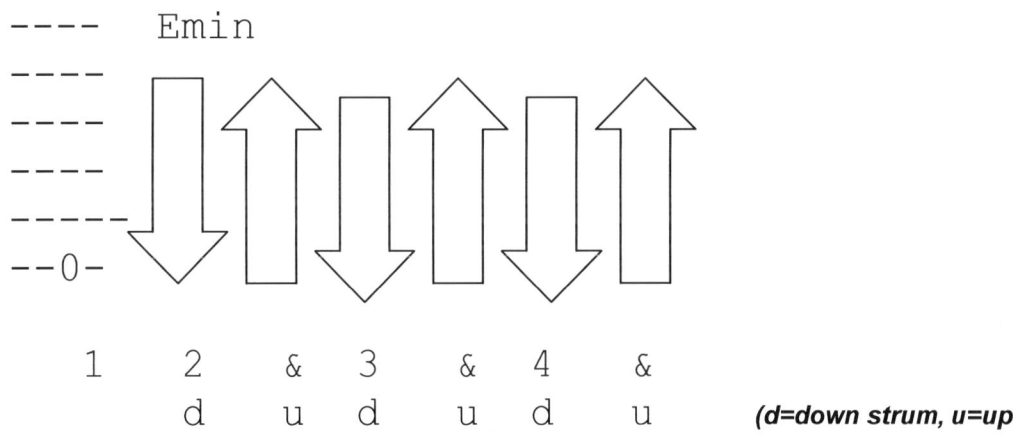

(d=down strum, u=up strum)

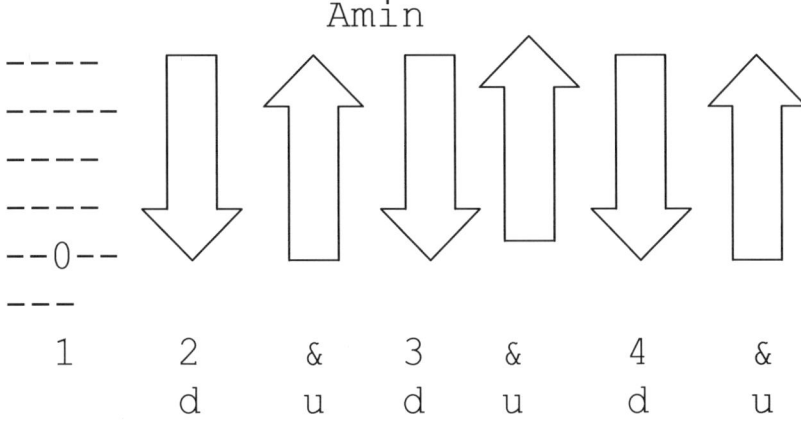

0= means to hit the 5th or A sting open

Lesson 6

Now form the emin then the aminor and do a
new chord a d7

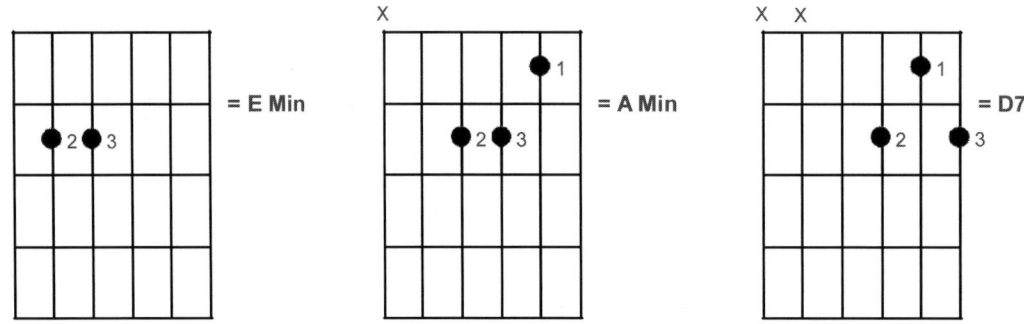

Strum straight down

    emin   amin   d7   G
    4x   4x   4x   4x

Lesson 7

Do You Remember C and G

G	emin	C	D7	G
8x	8x	4x	4x	8x

Strumming first strum down down down down in quarter notes

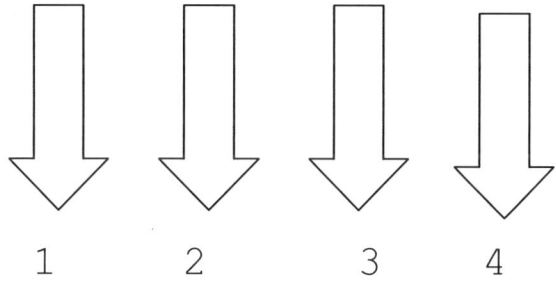

1 2 3 4

2nd strum down strum down down up down down up eighth notes are two beats for every one like the high hat on standard 4/4 beat

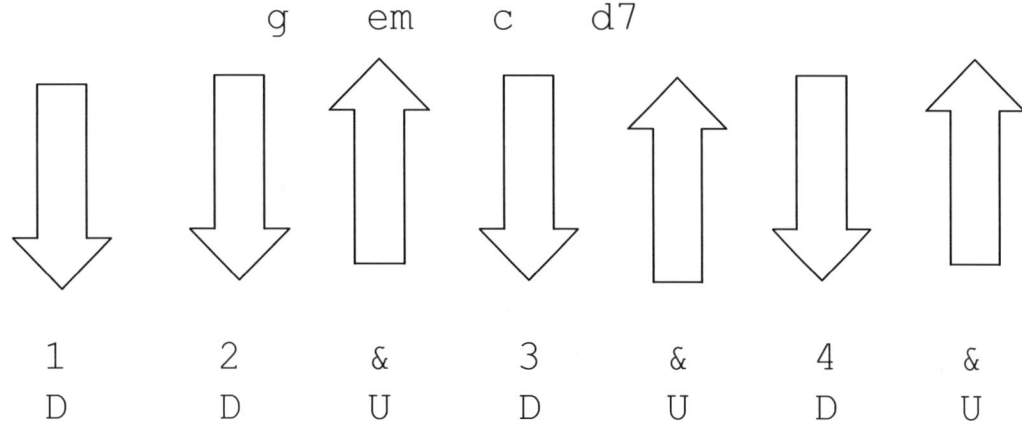

Lesson 8

Here's another set of chords stay with the fingering because A7 will lead to D

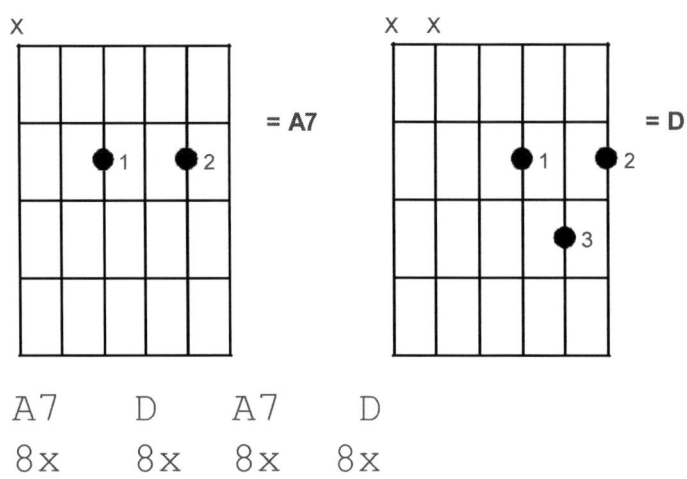

```
A7    D    A7    D
8x    8x   8x    8x
```

START ON THE D THIS TIME THEN GO To THE A7

```
D     A7    D     A     D
8x    8X    8x    4X    4X
```

COMBINE little G D AND A7

```
D    G    D    G    D    G    A7
4X   4x   4x   4x   4x   4x   8x
```

Lesson 9
AMAZING GRACE YOU'VE COME THIS FAR
Strum straight down in quarter notes

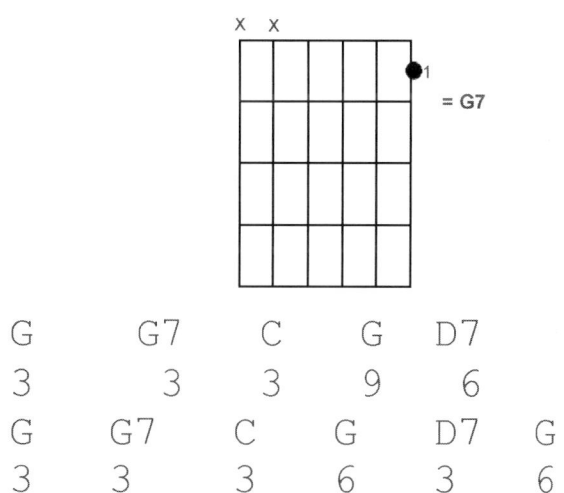

G	G7	C	G	D7	
3	3	3	9	6	
G	G7	C	G	D7	G
3	3	3	6	3	6

Lesson 10 em7 A
Strum straight down in quarter notes

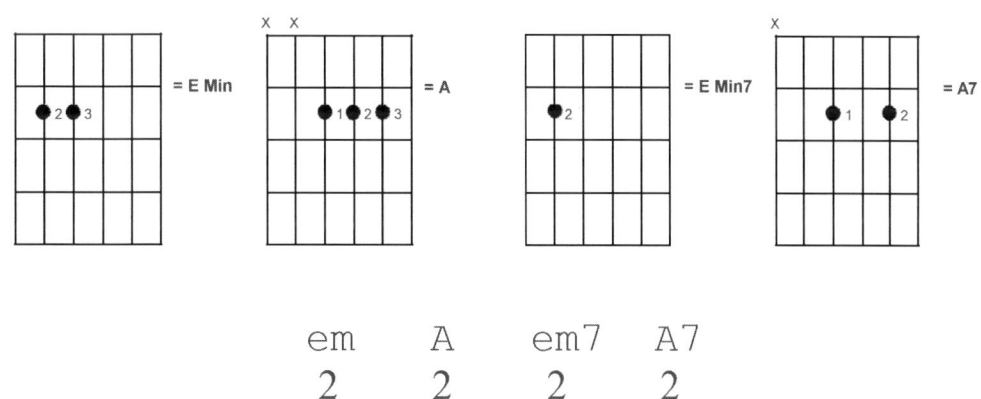

em	A	em7	A7
2	2	2	2

Lesson 11 Full C and G

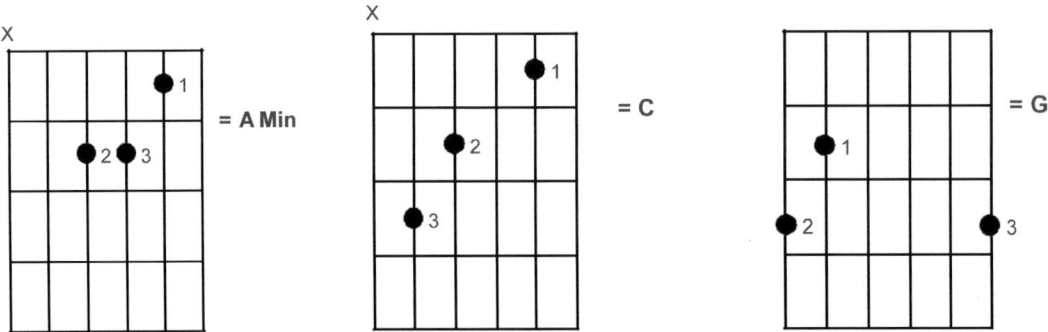

The way I would like you to learn your Full C chord is strum straight down on the A Minor and move one finger to make it a C.

```
Amin    C
 4      4
```

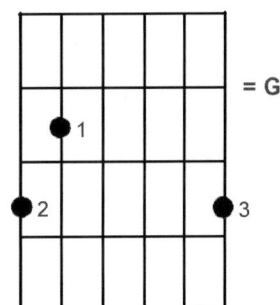

Strum straight down on C and G.

```
C   G   C
8   8   8
```

Now using your full chords strum the following exercise:
Strum straight down with quarter notes

```
G       Emin    C       D7      G
8       8       4       4       8
```

Lesson 12 A TEST OF YOUR CHORDS

Strum straight down with quarter notes and use either the small C, G and G7 or the full chord. Whatever you feel comfortable with.

G	D	Emin	A	A7	D	D7
4	4	8	4	4	4	4

G	D	emin	G7
4	4	4	4

C	G	D7	G
8	4	4	1

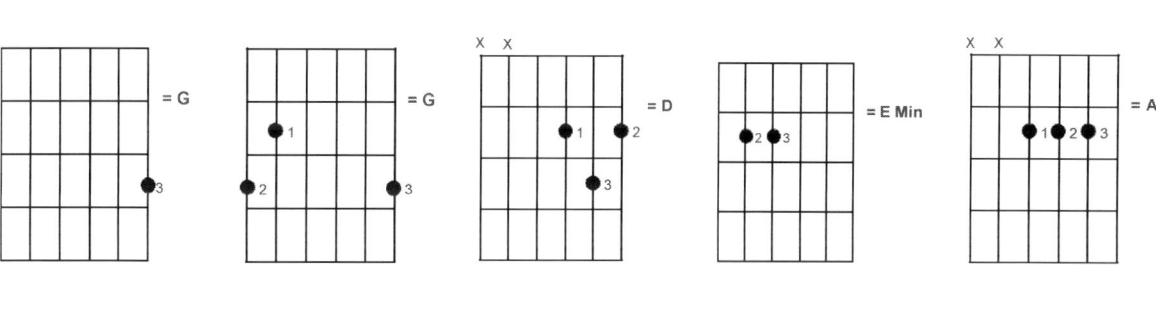

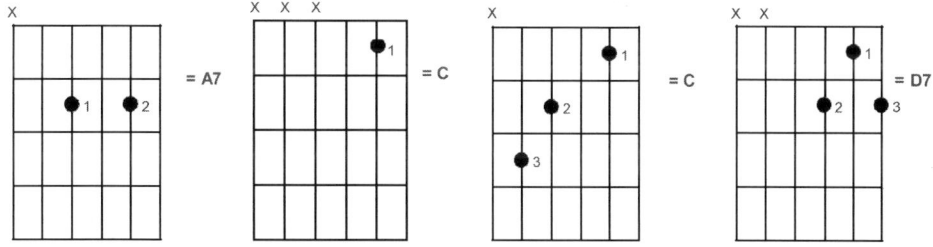

And here is a new version of a G7

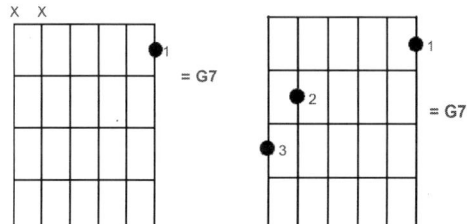

Lesson 13 Bminor sub

Move your amin up two frets I use this with beginning students to help them be introduced to a bminor chord

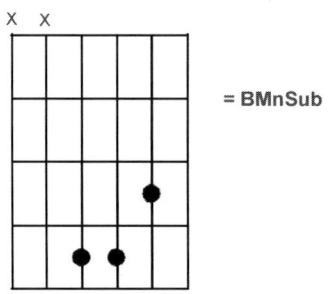

```
Ex1.  amin     bmin sub     C      bmin sub
       2x         2x        2x        2x
```

Lesson 14 B7

Here's a new chord a B7 ...If you look at the B7 part of the chord has a little form of a d7 in it. Strum Straight Down on these chords

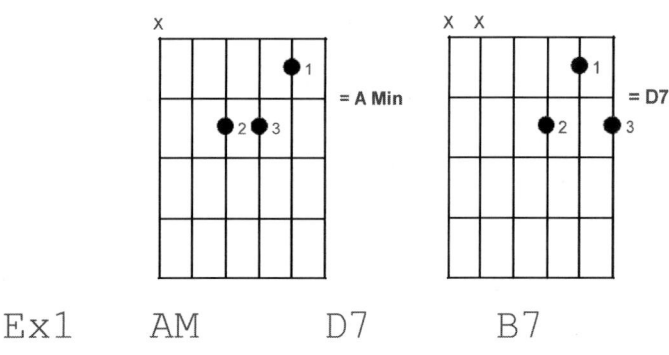

```
Ex1    AM     D7     B7
4x     4x     4x     4x
```

Lesson 15 A and E

E Chord is just like and aminor except on the lower strings or 1 more note than an eminor

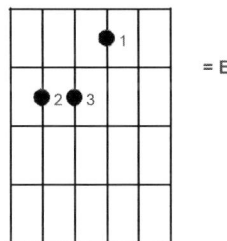

Try this AA   DD   EE   DD

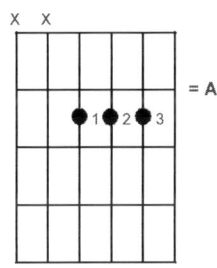 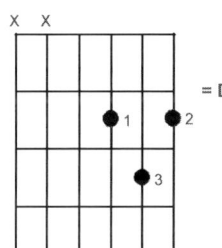 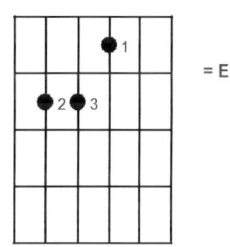

Lesson 16

Lets combine some of the chords we've learned and add one new chord an F#7

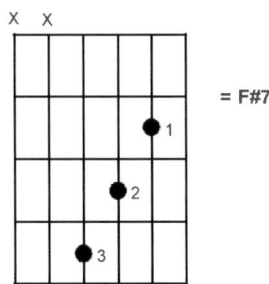

```
bminsub  F#7        A       E
8        8          8       8


G        D          Em      f#7
8        8          8       8
```

Lesson 17 Power Chords

The first time I ever heard power chords was in the 60's when I first heard "You Really Got Me. At that time, power chords were bar chords that went up the scale chromatically. The chromatic scale is nothing more than the 12-tone order of notes:

 # Sharp raises the note
b Flat lowers the note
A note between a C and a D is called a C# or a Db (Some notes have two names)

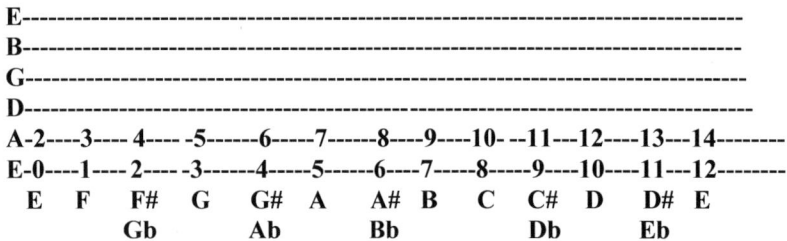

If you barred your **E** chord, you could get a set of power chords and if you barred your **A** you could get a set of chords.

```
E-------------------------------------------------------------------
B-------------------------------------------------------------------
G-------------------------------------------------------------------
D-2-----3-----4-----5-----6-----7-----8-----9-----10----11----12-----13---- 14
A-0-----1-----2-----3-----4-----5-----6-----7-----8-----9-----10-----11---- 12
E-------------------------------------------------------------------
  A  A#   B   C   C#   D   D#   E   F   F#   G   G#   A
     Bb       Db       Eb           Gb       Ab
```

The whole chord used to be played with the emphasis on the lower note, that is called the root note, and fifth notes of the chord. Usually, a band would have one guitar play the power chord and another guitar play the same guitar chord in another position.

What modern alternative and heavy metal has done in many cases is drop the four strings of the bar chord and just play what is called the root and the fifth. So, if you are playing your power chord on the third fret, you are playing a **G5** or a **G** with a fifth.

A chord is a combination of three notes in harmony. A G chord would be a: **G - B and D** note. A **G - MINOR** notes are: **G - Bb and D**. So, in a sense, a modern power chord is neither major or minor. The chord progression in the song can suggest what key you are in, or, if to use a major or minor scale with the power chord. But, technically speaking, a power chord is neither major or minor.

A chord is made up of a: **1st, 3rd, and 5th** of a musical scale.
Example: **C MAJOR SCALE: C - D - E - F - G - A - B - C**
   (CEG) (DFA) (EGB) (FAC) (GBD) (ACE) (BDF) are all chords.....

It is also important to know where to put your scales....A power chord in **A** could use the blues scale on the fifth fret, the major scale, minor scale, or mode on the fifth fret.

Just for the record, punk and heavy metal were not the first to use a root and a fifth together as a chord...it was used in medieval music for background accompaniment.
You may also go up the scale with barred minor 7ths, major 7ths, 6ths, and ninth chords.

Lesson 18 and 19

To make a long story short, your basic chords that you learn in the beginning of your guitar lessons can be moved up and down the guitar. Your D - Dm - F - Fm - Bb - Bm - and - D7 all can be moved according to the chromatic scale. Your chromatic scale is nothing more than the order of the notes .

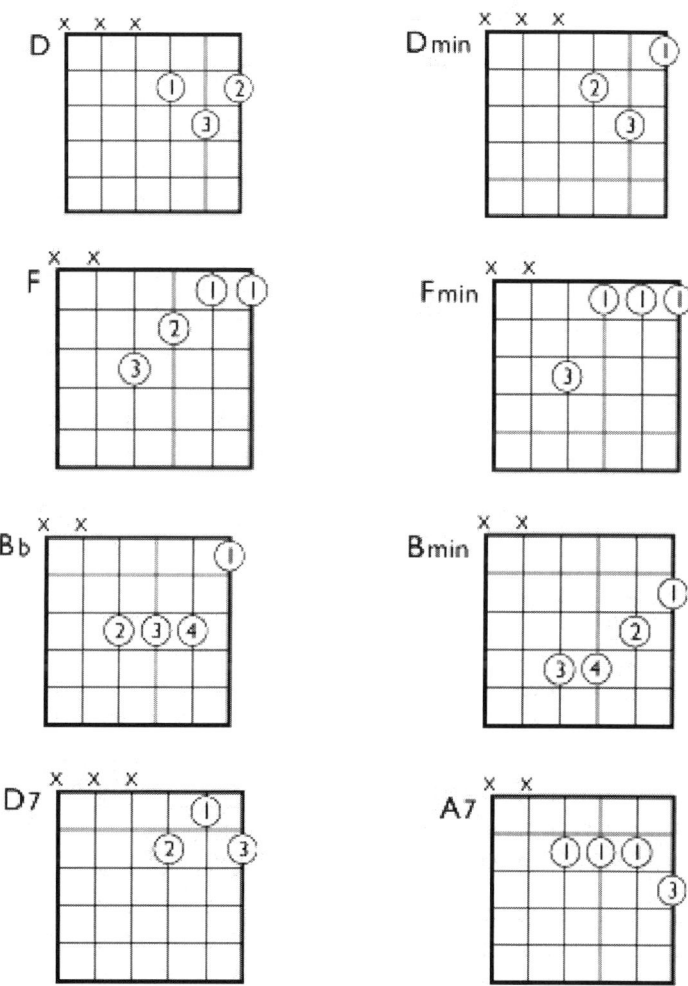

The Chromatic Scale Is:

C C# D D# E F F# G G# A A# B (then back to C)
   Db   Eb   Gb   Ab   Bb

Some notes have two names - C# is the same as Db and etc.
Another way of memorizing this scale would be to say there is a sharp or flat between all notes except E and F and B and C. Actually your whole guitar works this way. Your individual notes go up the strings in the same way.
Below are the names of your strings:

6 5 4 3 2 1
E A D G B E

Your notes go up the scale in the same way. It is important to know your note names, for when you learn your scales, if you know your note names you will be able to play the scales all over the guitar.

It is important when you move up the scale with your chords not to hit any notes that have an X over them. Moving these chords around will save you alot of time and also will enable you to play thousands of more songs than if you just knew your chords in the first position.

To have a good knowledge of chords is important because it gives you more variety in chord sounds and also many lead guitar players build their leads with and around chords.

If you take for example your D chord in the first position and compare it to the D chord in the Bb position you will see the order of notes in the D chord in the first position is: D - A - D and F#. If you look at the order of notes in the Bb position of the D chord, you will see the order of the notes is (if barred): D - A - D - F# and A. If you play a D in the first position and go to G, your top melody note will go from F# to G. If you play D (in the Bb position), your top notes will go from A to G. This might sound small but these variations in chords are the basis of harmony and composition. It also gives other melodies in your soloing and chording.

These chords move up and down the guitar..You can either learn this system and learn the chords or look into a chord book and try to figure out thousands of chords.. To learn the chords you will be able to see the pattern of the guitar.

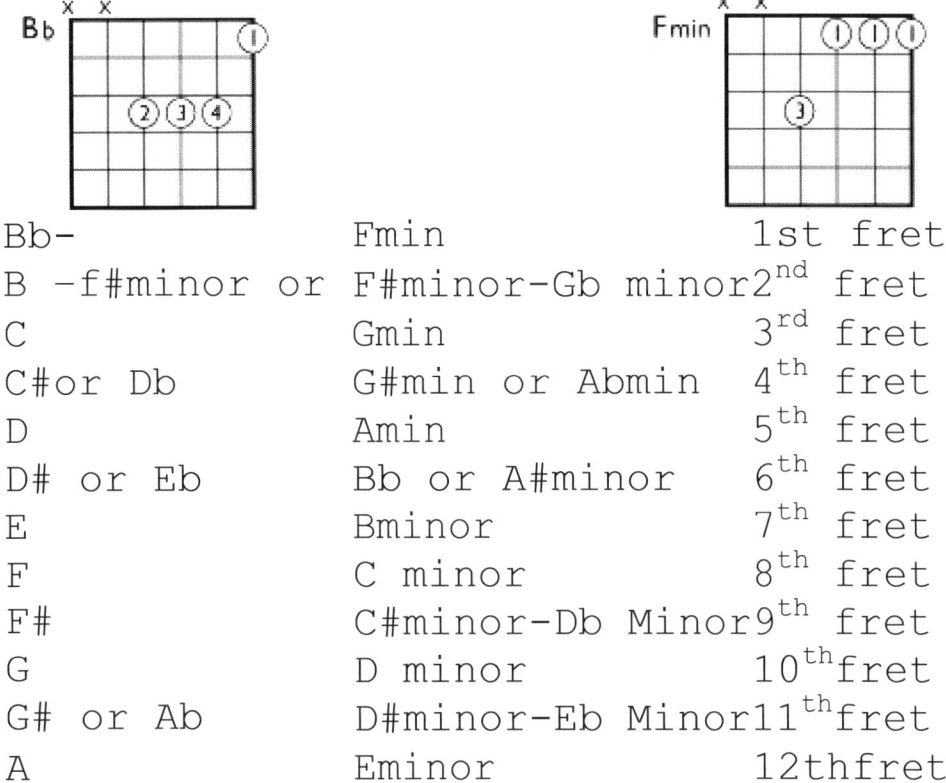

Bb-	Fmin	1st fret
B -f#minor or	F#minor-Gb minor	2nd fret
C	Gmin	3rd fret
C#or Db	G#min or Abmin	4th fret
D	Amin	5th fret
D# or Eb	Bb or A#minor	6th fret
E	Bminor	7th fret
F	C minor	8th fret
F#	C#minor-Db Minor	9th fret
G	D minor	10th fret
G# or Ab	D#minor-Eb Minor	11th fret
A	Eminor	12th fret

These are movable Chords up and down the guitar. The shape of the chord stays the same but the name changes when you move it up and down the fretboard.

A major chord such as an F chord will either be called F or Fmajor or Fmaj.

A minor chord will be called for example either eminor or emin or em.

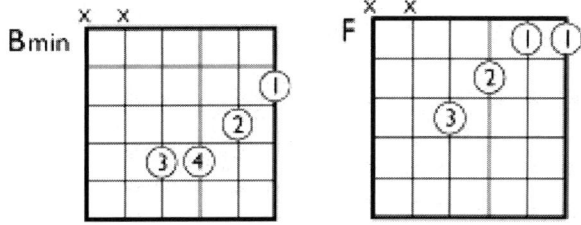

Movable Bminor and F

Bbminor-A#minor	F	1st fret
B minor -	F# or Gb	2nd fret
C minor	G	3rd fret
C#minor-Dbminor	G# or Ab	4th fret
D min	A	5th fret
D#min-Ebminor	A# or Bb	6th fret
E minor	B	7th fret
F minor	C	8th fret
F#minor-Gbminor	C# or Db	9th fret
G minor	D	10th fret
G#minor-Abminor	D# or Eb	11th fret
A minor	E	12th fret

These are also movable chords
The principles of these chords moving around will also apply to other chords as well, such as 7ths and 9ths.

Chord Variations:
```
D, Dsus4, Dsus2, Asus2, Asus4, Dmin, F, Fmajor7, F6, F7
```

Variations of the D chord:

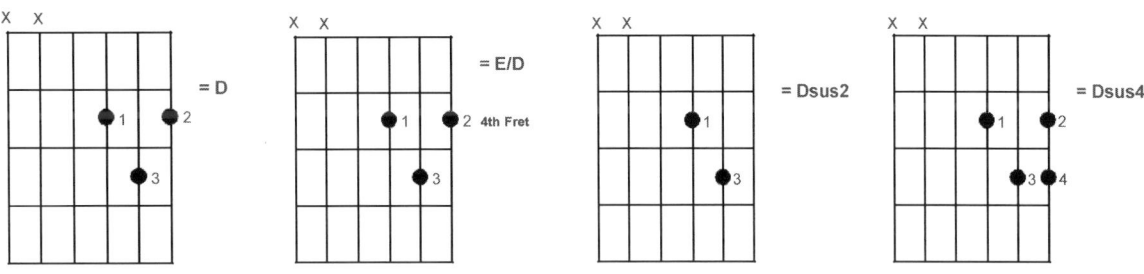

Variations of the A chord:

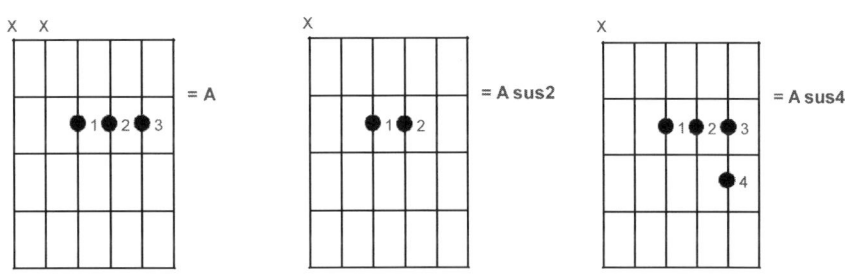

New chord Dminor:

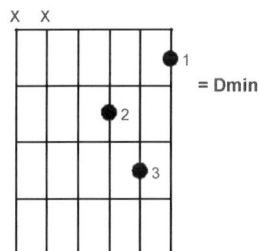

Variations of the F chord:

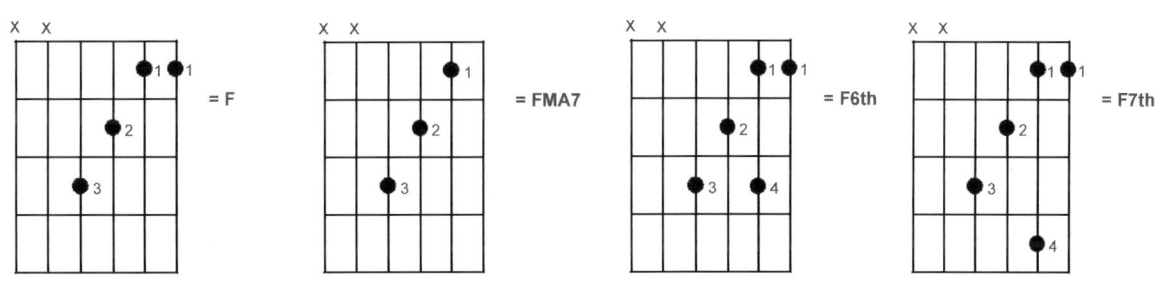

Chord Exercises

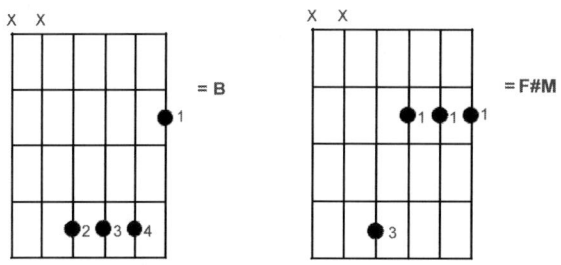

```
Ex 1:E  B  A  E   F#M  A   E:
     4  4  4  4    4   4   8
```

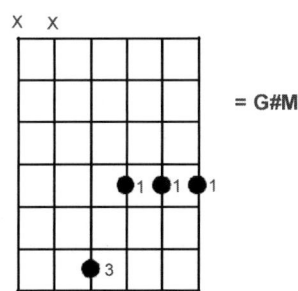

```
                    Exercise 2  G#M A G#M A
G#M F#M B
```

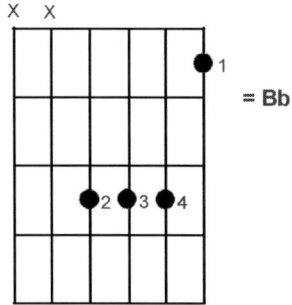

```
:DMIN  Bb  C  DMIN:
   4    4  4   4
```

Extra lessons

Here are a couple of my songs that I think will help your guitar playing. You can hear these songs on You Tube and Spotify or purchase them at I Tunes or CD Baby.

Where are We Going?
Strum straight down two beats on each of the chords

Whiskey Island-Once again strum straight down two beats on each chord

Environmental Girlfriend -
The number of strums with this power chord exercise is on top of the page
Strum straight down on 8th notes

I Can See A Rainbow- This is a little tricky but strum this one and pay attention to what fingers to use on these chords. If you get really stuck just use a simpler G D Em and C.

Hopefully   I helped you get going on the guitar and I hope you keep playing.

Where are we Going?   CP   Dennis Carleton

```
G          D         C         G         G         D       C         G
Talk about misdirection I see it all around me,  People are rushing to and fro
G          D        C           G    -       G       D         C
Give me the time, give me the season , When people had a reason  to know
              G
what they know

 G         D        C         G   Emin      C    D       G
Where are we going? Where are we going? Where are we going? I'd like to know

 G      D       C         G       G        D           C         G
60's was one thing 70's was another, all through the ages it's been love your brother
G           D          C            G            D
We run away from love , we run away from the reign ,it's always a battle
         C        G
tween Able and Cain

 G         D        C         G   Emin      C    D       G
Where are we going? Where are we going? Where are we going? I'd like to know

 G      D       C         G       G        D           C         G
50's was one thing 60's was another, all through the ages it's been love your brother
G           D          C            G       G      D      C
We run away from love , we run away from the reign ,somehow science don't
        G
help me stay sane (

 G         D        C         G   Emin      C    D       G
Where are we going? Where are we going?  Where are we going? I'd like to know

G          D        C           G       G        D            C
Apes they are talking, computers play chess, The  Book of Revelations is  anyone's
G
guess
G          D        C         G      G                    D
Women are working, and man is at rest and when they're going to clone they're
         C       G
going to use the best     (

 G         D        C         G   Emin      C    D       G
Where are we going? Where are we going? Where are we going? Only God knows
```

Whiskey Island   CP Dennis Carleton

Em   C   D   Em   Em   D   Amin   B7
The story I tell, a hidden mystery of people rocks and sand,
Em   D   C   Em   Am   Em   B7   Em
Steel and salt, nature flowing free hear the tale of Whiskey Island

Em   C   D   Em   Em   D   Amin   B7
Lorenzo Carter, was the first to settle there, then came Dave and Gilman Bryant Whiskey Island
Em   D   C   Emin   Amin   Em   B7 Emin
Distilled whiskey fought mosquitoes and snakes, thus came Whiskey Island

Em   C   D   Em   Em   D   Amin   B7
Then came the Irish, who lived and lie there, they struggled to make a dollar
Em   D   C   Em   Em   D   Amin   B7
They worked real hard, Sunday went to church, hooray for Whiskey Island

Em   C   D   Em   Em   D   Amin   B7
Railyards ,factories ,steam driven ships,changing the Island forever
Em   D   C   Em   Am   Em   B7   Em
Shanties of tar and tin in the great depression Hooverville on Whiskey Island

Em   C   D   Em   Em   D   Amin   B7
Queen Ann's Lace, willows to the north, cottonwood, doves and swan
Em   D   C   Em   Am   Em   B7   Em
Sunfish pond, Monarch Butterfly, exist on Whiskey Island

Em   C   D   Em   Em   D   Amin   B7
Woods and weeds, dogs and deer   seagulls circle the station
Em   D   C   Em   Am   Em   B7   Em
The Coast Guard's pride,broken men have called home,here on Whiskey Island

Em   C   D   Em   Em   D   Amin   B7
Moonscape of sand dunes, rock piles to the south , 600 miles of   salt   mines
Em   D   C   Em   Am   Emin   B7   Em
Dinosaur Hullets, add to the ambience , pyramids on Whiskey   Island

Environmental Girlfriend—Power chord exercise
Chord Pattern

```
E5  A5  B5   E5  A5  B5  E5 B5    E5 A5 B5   A5 B5    E5 A5    A5 B5   E5 A5 E5 B5
 8   4   4    8   2   2   2  2     8  4  4    4  4     4  4     4  4    2  2  2  2

E-----------------------------------------------------------------------
B-----------------------------------------------------------------------
G-----------------------------------------------------------------------
D -9-- -----2---------4-------------------------------------------------
A -7-- -----0---------2-----------2-------------7---------9-----
E -0-----------------------------------0------------5---------7-----
    E5      A5        B5            E5          A5         B5
```

Environmental Girlfriend

```
 E5                              A5                  B5
We'll sit around and talk about the ozone and how the world might end
 E5                              A5       B5   E5 B5
We'll separate and sort all our trash right into the recycle bin
 E5                              A5              B
But the way you sort through all that waste I know were more than friends
         A5           B5              E5                A5
It's not the way you look, or the way you cook, it's the way you think that nature spins
         A5          B5           A5          B5    E5 B5
It's an all natural love sent from above my environmental girlfriend
```

Verse 2
We will protect our habitat, but not because it's a trend. We' balance our checks in the balance of life, We'll watch what we spend We'll recycle our glass and our memories and the cycle will never end. It's not the way you look or the way you cook it's the way you think that nature spins. It's an all natural love sent from above my environmental girlfriend

Verse 3
We'll read our letters from our congressman from the letters that we send. We'll take our stance with the plants and trees but we will never bend. We'll speak for those who can not speak it's those we will defend. It's not the way you look or the way you cook it's the way you think that nature spins it's an all natural love sent from above my environmental girlfriend.

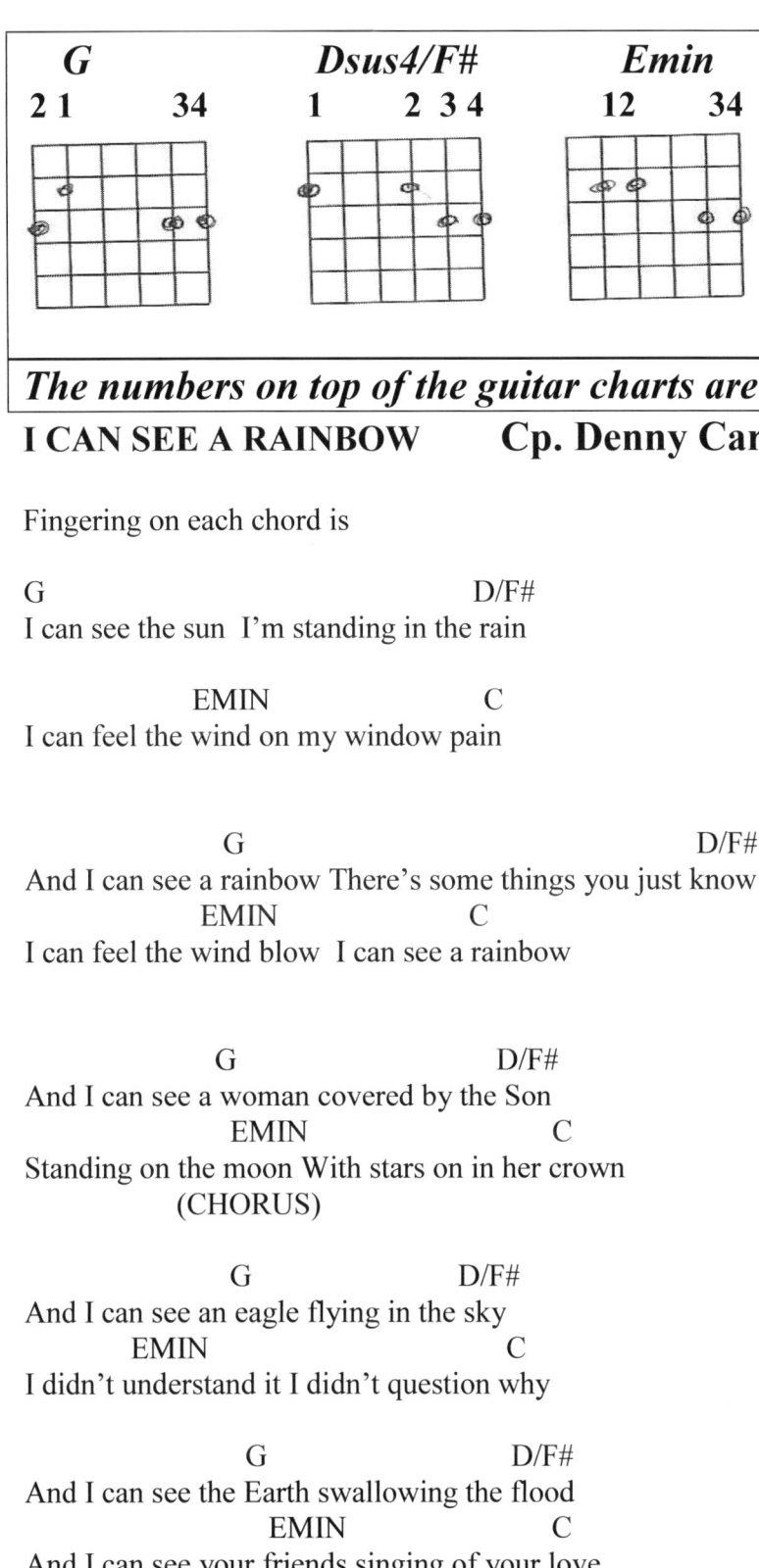

The numbers on top of the guitar charts are what fingers to use

I CAN SEE A RAINBOW   Cp. Denny Carleton

Fingering on each chord is

G   D/F#
I can see the sun I'm standing in the rain

         EMIN   C
I can feel the wind on my window pain

         G   D/F#
And I can see a rainbow There's some things you just know
         EMIN   C
I can feel the wind blow I can see a rainbow

         G   D/F#
And I can see a woman covered by the Son
              EMIN   C
Standing on the moon With stars on in her crown
         (CHORUS)

         G   D/F#
And I can see an eagle flying in the sky
         EMIN   C
I didn't understand it I didn't question why

         G   D/F#
And I can see the Earth swallowing the flood
                EMIN   C
And I can see your friends singing of your love

         (CHORUS)

25

Made in the USA
Middletown, DE
28 September 2022